SUCCOTH

A JOYOUS HOLIDAY

A Storybook
with
Activities

Written and Illustrated by
Barbara Soloff-Levy

Watermill Press
© 1991 by Watermill Press, Mahwah, N.J. All rights reserved.

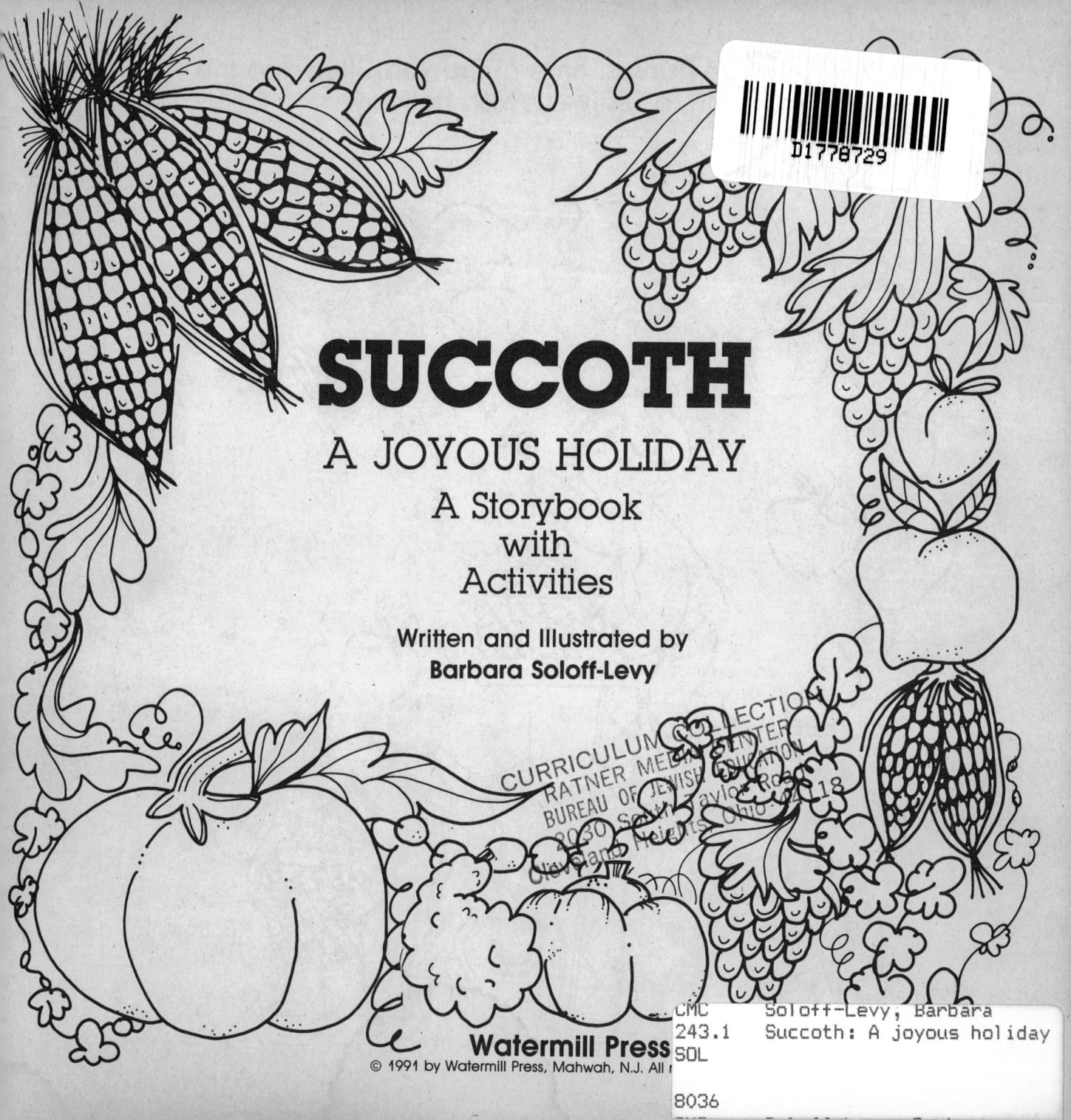

Early fall is the harvest time of the year. It is also the time of Succoth, a festive Jewish holiday.

Follow the dots

At this time of the year, we gather fruits and vegetables from the garden.

The earth gives us a harvest of delicious food. Here are some of the vegetables, fruits, and grains from the fall harvest. Unscramble their names and color them.

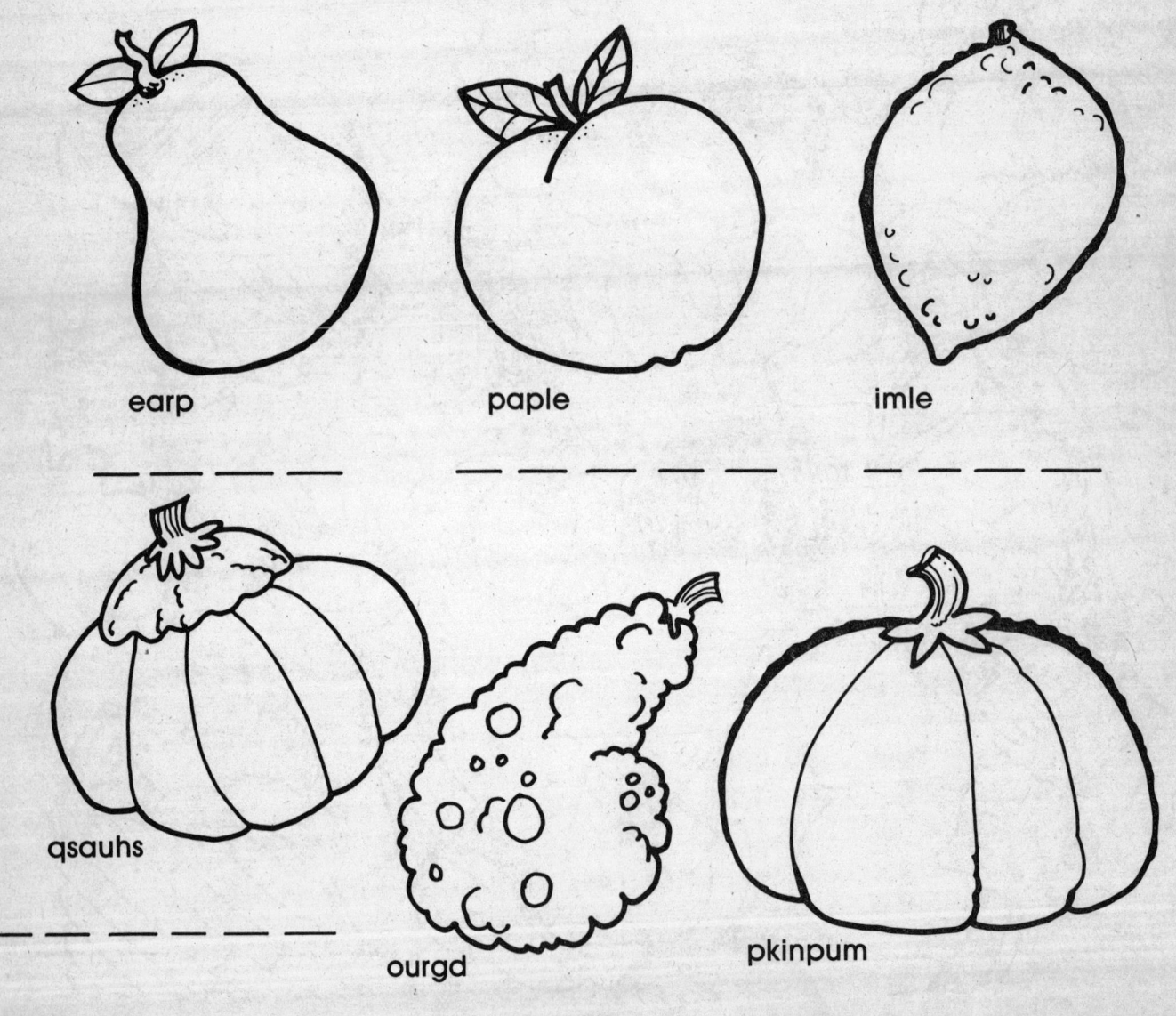

We are thankful for all the earth has given us.
Succoth is a time to give thanks for our food.

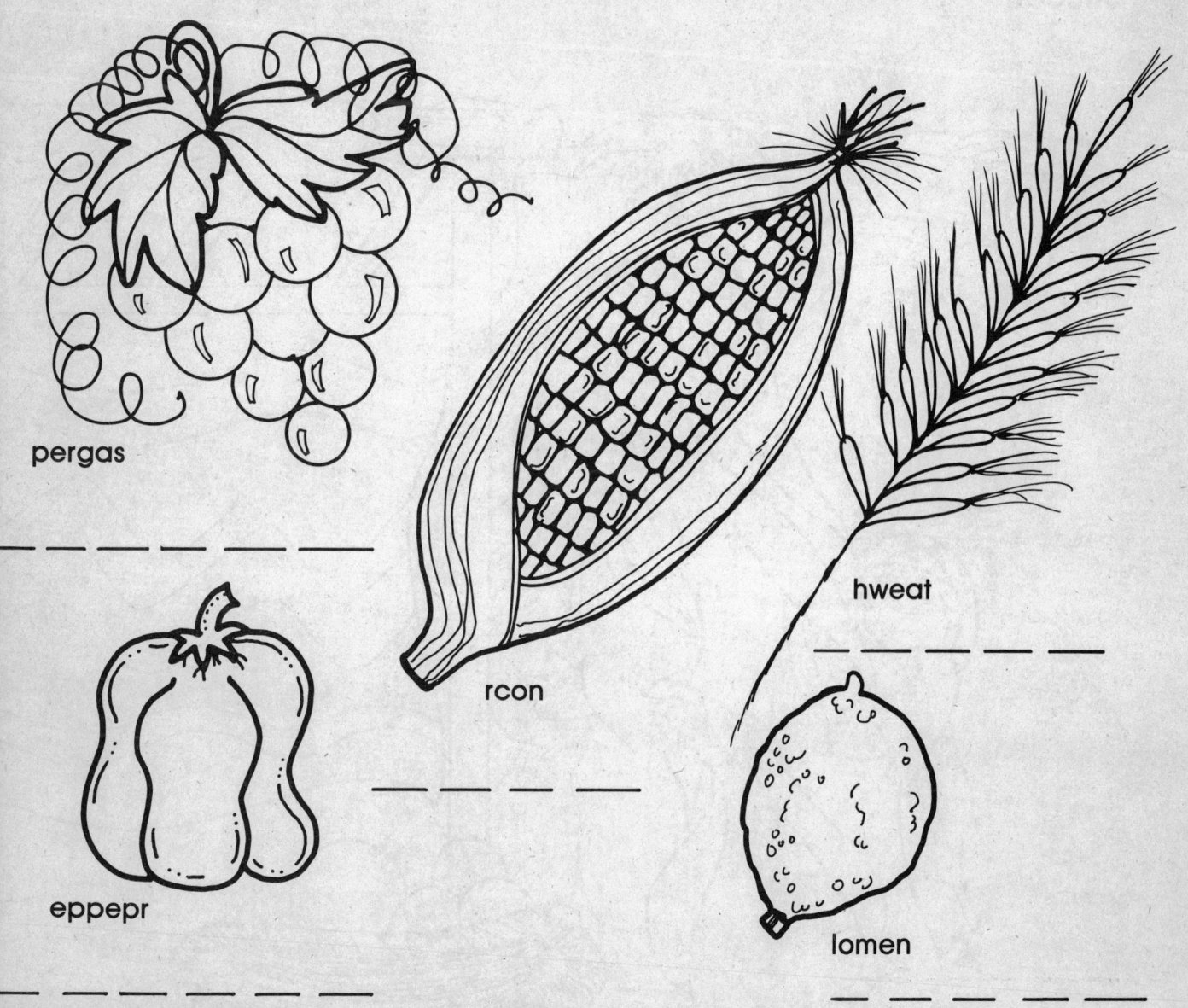

Succoth started long ago when the Jewish people escaped from slavery. They traveled through the desert for forty years, looking for a home. While they were in the desert, they lived in huts called Succah.

The people slept and ate in their Succahs. Every time they moved to a new place, they took their Succahs with them.

Finally, people settled in a place called Canaan. Here, they farmed the land. Their fields were far away from their homes.

Once again, they built huts to eat and sleep in near their crops.

Today, Succahs are a symbol of the past. Some are built with wood.

Wire mesh holds decorations. The roof is sometimes made of twigs and branches, so the stars can shine in.

Fruits and vegetables decorate the Succah and are a reminder of the harvest.

Children make different crafts to hang on the walls.

Succoth lasts eight days. Some families eat all their meals in the Succah during the holiday.

Two symbols of the harvest are the *etrog* and the *lulav*.

The *etrog* is a sweet-smelling fruit. It stands for the fruit of the tree. It is also a symbol of the heart.

The *lulav* is a palm tied with myrtle and willow twigs. It stands for the spine, eyes, and lips. Together, the *lulav* and *etrog* are symbols of the body and the soul.

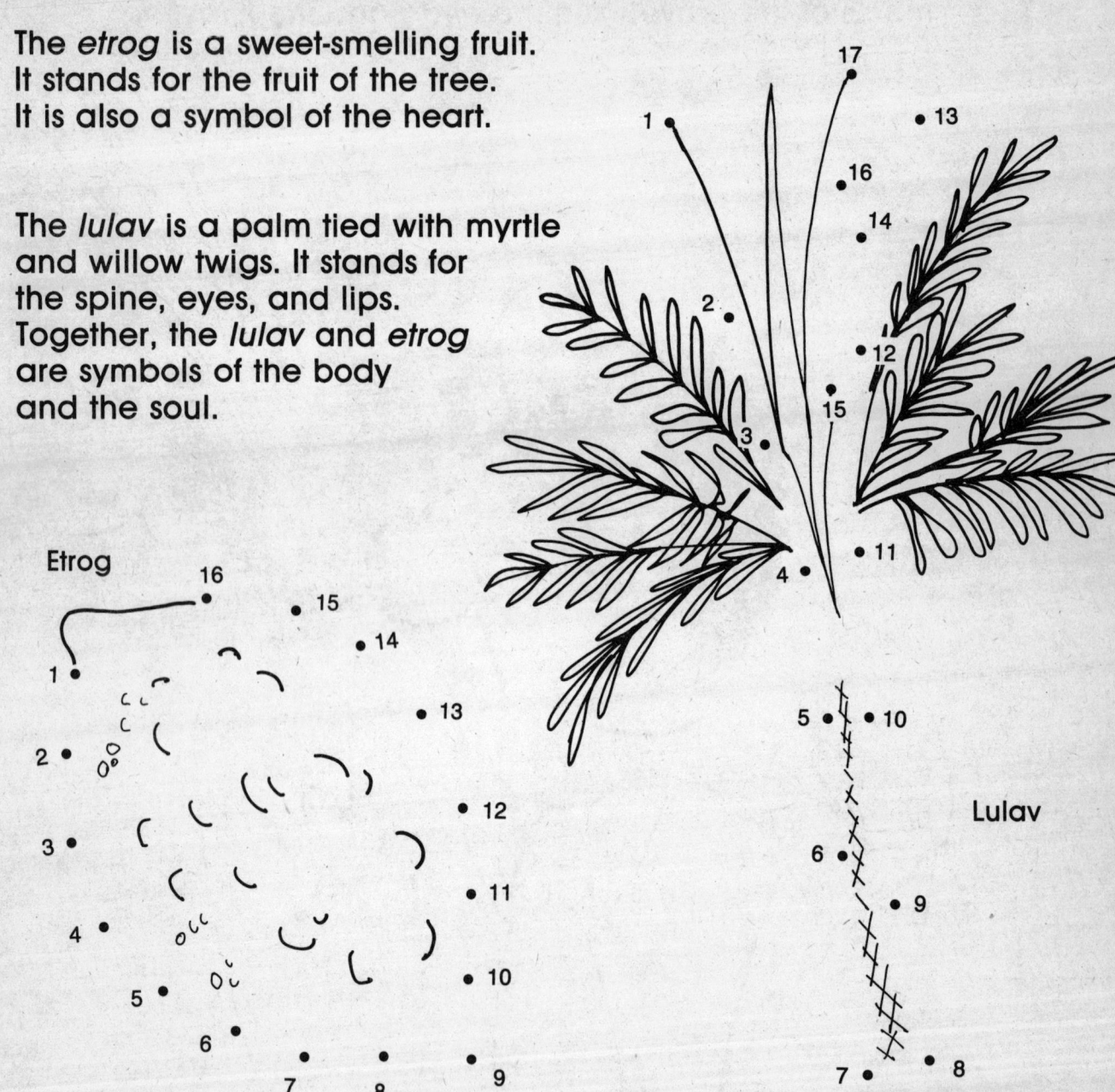

Families and friends go to the synagogue to celebrate Succoth together.

After the service, everyone goes to the Succah to eat delicious treats. It is fun to celebrate this wonderful holiday!

Some Facts about Succoth

The Succah is a temporary shelter. It shows us that we should not depend on material things, because they are temporary, too. Instead, we should depend on faith in God.

Succahs are also a link with the past. When people sit in the Succah, they remember the Jewish people of long ago who did the same thing.

Here are some ways to decorate your Succah:

Trace or copy these fruits and vegetables and color them. Then cut them out and paste them on cardboard. Punch a hole on the dotted circle and tie a string through the hole to hang up your drawings.

To protect your fruits and vegetables from the rain, cover them with plastic wrap.

Chains Make Good Decorations

Paper Chains
You will need: colored paper, glue, scissors. Cut the paper into 7" strips. Roll the strips into circles and link them together to make a chain.

Popcorn Chains

You will need: popcorn, needle, thread. Pop the corn. String the popcorn onto a long piece of thread by pulling the needle through the thick part of the popcorn.

Cranberry Chains

You will need: cranberries, needle, thread. String the cranberries onto a long piece of thread.
You can also mix popcorn and cranberries to make popcorn-cranberry chains.

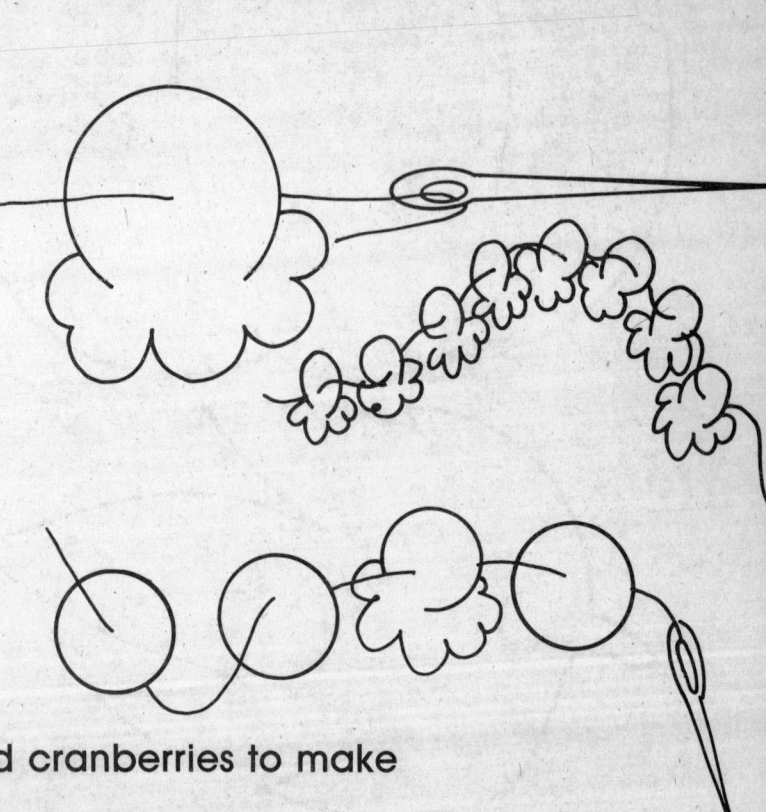

A Mobile is Fun

Here's how to make a mobile to hang in your Succah: You will need: dried corn, dried peas, different kinds of dried beans, pen or pencil, cardboard, scissors, hole punch, string, glue, wire hanger.

1. Trace or copy the apple on p. 20 onto a piece of cardboard and cut it out. Repeat until you have several apples.
2. Punch a hole on the dotted circle and tie a string through it to hang each apple.
3. Cover one side of each cardboard apple with glue.
4. Place the beans, corn, and peas on each apple. Make any kind of design you like. Let the glue dry.
5. Tie the apples onto the wire hanger so they hang at different lengths. Hang your mobile from the roof of your Succah, or hang it in your room.

Welcome!

Every Succah should have a sign of welcome over the door. Here are two signs you can make. Trace the letters and pictures on a piece of cardboard and cover it with plastic to protect it from the rain. You can also glue your sign to a piece of wood. Then hang it over the door to welcome friends and family.

This is the Hebrew word for "Welcome."

Shalom means "Hello," "Good-bye," and "Peace." Color the letters, or fill them in with dried beans.

SHALOM